Content

LIST OF FIGURES

1. INTRODUCTION

As XML becomes a predominant means of linking blocks of information together, there is a requirement to secure specific information. That is to allow authorized entities access to specific information and prevent access to that specific information from unauthorized entities. Current methods on the Internet include password protection, smart card, PKI, tokens and a variety of other schemes. These typically solve the problem of accessing the site from unauthorized users, but do not provide mechanisms for the protection of specific information from all those who have authorized access to the site.

Now that XML is being used to provide searchable and organized information there is a sense of urgency to provide a standard to protect certain parts or elements from unauthorized access. The objective of XML encryption is to provide a standard methodology that prevents unauthorized access to specific information within an XML document.

2. INTRODUCTION TO XML

XML (Extensible Markup Language) was developed by an XML Working Group (originally known as the SGML Editorial Review Board) formed under the auspices of the World Wide Web Consortium (W3C) in 1996. Even though there was HTML, DHTML and SGML XML was developed byW3C to achieve the following design goals.

- XML shall be straightforwardly usable over the Internet.

- XML shall be compatible with SGML.

- It shall be easy to write programs, which process XML documents.

- The design of XML shall be formal and concise.

- XML documents shall be easy to create.

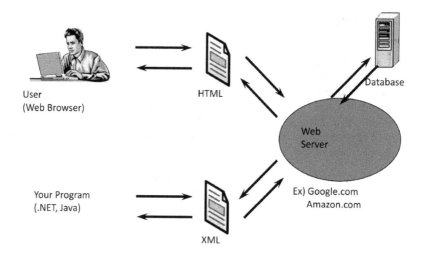

Figure 1: Xml web services

2.1 Why XML?

XML was created so that richly structured documents could be used over the web. The other alternate is HTML and SGML are not practical for this purpose.HTML comes bound with a set of semantics and does not provide any arbitrary structure. Even though SGML provides arbitrary structure, it is too difficult to implement just for web browser. Since SGML is so comprehensive that only large corporations can justify the cost of its implementations.

2.2 XML Definition

The eXtensible Markup Language, abbreviated as XML, describes a class of data objects called XML documents and partially describes the behavior of computer programs which process them. Thus XML is a restricted form of SGML

2.3 Documents

A data object is an XML document if it is well-formed, as defined in this specification. A well-formed XML document may in addition be valid if it meets certain further constraints. Each XML document has both a logical and a physical structure. Physically, the document is composed of units called entities. An entity may refer to other entities to cause their inclusion in the document. A document begins in a "root" or document entity.

A textual object is a well-formed XML document if It meets all the well-forkedness' constraints :Each of the parsed entities which is referenced directly or indirectly within the document is well-formed.

    Document   ::= Prolog element Misc*

2.4 Element Type Declarations

The element structure of an XML document may, for validation purposes, be constrained using element type and attribute-list declarations. An element type declaration constrains the element's content. Element type declarations often constrain which element types can appear as children of the element. At user option, an XML processor may issue a warning when a declaration mentions an element type for which no declaration is provided, but this is not an error.

Element Type Declaration

    elementdecl ::= '<!ELEMENT' Name contentspec ? '>'

    contentspec ::= 'EMPTY' | 'ANY' | Mixed | children

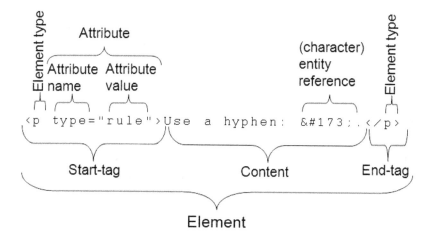

Figure 2: Anatomy of an element

XML is a major enabler of what the Internet, and latterly Web services, require to continue growing and developing. Yet a lot of work remains to be done on security-related issues before the full capabilities of XML languages can be realized. Traditional methods of establishing trust between parties aren't appropriate on the public Internet or, indeed, on large LANs or WANs. There are particular difficulties in dealing with hierarchical data structures and with subsets of data with varying requirements as to confidentiality, access authority, or integrity. In addition, the application of new standard security controls differentially to XML documents is not at all straightforward.

At present, encrypting a complete XML document, testing its integrity, and confirming the authenticity of its sender is a straightforward process. But it is increasingly necessary to use these functions on parts of documents, to encrypt and authenticate in arbitrary sequences, and to involve different users or originators. At present, the most important sets of developing specifications in the area of XML-related security are XML encryption, XML signature; XACL, SAML, and XKMS This article introduces XML encryption and XML signature.

• Stego.6te.net GoogleBrowser

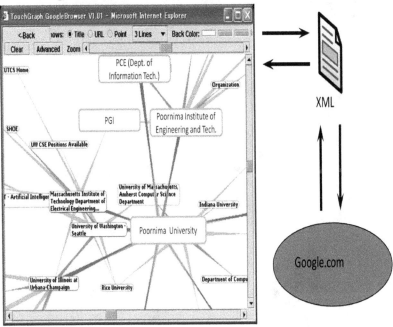

Figure 3:- XWS Application Examples

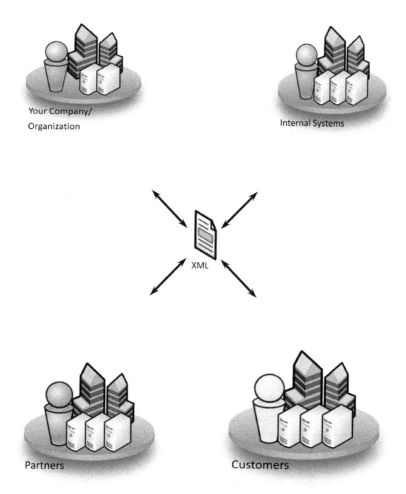

Figure 4:- System Integration with XWS

3. ENCRYPTION

Encryption: This ensures that your data was unable to be read or utilized by any party while in transit. Your message is encrypted into incomprehensible gibberish before it leaves your computer. It maintains it encrypted (gibberish) state during it's travel through the Internet. It is not de-crypt until the recipient receives it. Because of the public-key cryptography used (discussed later) only the recipient can decipher the received message, no one else can.

3.1 How does it all work?

To understand how this all works, we need to start with the basics. Encryption has been around for centuries; Julius Caesar used encrypted notes to communicate with Rome thousands of years ago. This traditional cryptography is based on the sender and receiver of a message knowing and using the same secret key: the sender uses the secret key to encrypt the message, and the receiver uses the same secret key to decrypt the message. 21 years ago, a revolution happened in cryptography that changed all this, public-key cryptography. In 1976, Whitfield Diffie and Martin Hellman, introduced this new method of encryption and key management. A public-key cryptosystem is a cryptographic system that uses a pair of unique keys (a public key and a private key). Each individual is assigned a pair of these keys to encrypt and decrypt information. A message encrypted by one of these keys can only be decrypted by the other key in the pair.

The public key is available to others for use when encrypting information that will be sent to an individual. The private key is accessible only to the individual. The individual can use the private key to decrypt any messages encrypted with the public key. Similarly, the individual can use the private key to encrypt messages, so that the messages can only be decrypted with the corresponding public key.

Several bodies are actively involved in examining the issues and in developing standards. The main relevant developments here are XML encryption and the related XML signature, eXtensible Access Control Language (XACL), and the related Security.

4. ALGORITHMS AND STRUCTURES

4.1 Block Encryption Algorithms

Block encryption algorithms are designed for encrypting and decrypting data in fixed size, multiple octet blocks. Their identifiers appear as the value of the Algorithm attributes of EncryptionMethod elements that are children of EncryptedData. Block encryption algorithms take, as implicit arguments, the data to be encrypted or decrypted, the keying material, and their direction of operation. For all of these algorithms specified below, an initialization vector (IV) is required that is encoded with the cipher text.

4.1.1 Padding

Since the data being encrypted is an arbitrary number of octets, it may not be a multiple of the block size. This is solved by padding the plain text up to the block size before encryption and unpadding after decryption. The padding algorithm is to calculate the smallest non-zero number of octets, say N, that must be suffixed to the plain text to bring it up to a multiple of the block size. We will assume the block size is B octets so N is in the range of 1 to B. Pad by suffixing the plain text with N-1 arbitrary pad bytes and a final byte whose value is N. On decryption, just take the last byte and, after sanity checking it, strip that many bytes from the end of the decrypted cipher text.

For example, assume an 8 byte block size and plain text of 0x616263. The padded plain text would then be 0x616263????????05 where the "??" bytes can be any value.

4.2 Stream Encryption Algorithms

Simple stream encryption algorithms generate based on the key, a stream of bytes which are XORed with the plain text data bytes to produce the cipher text on encryption and with the cipher text bytes to produce plain text on decryption. They are normally used for the encryption of data and are specified by the value of the Algorithm attribute of the EncryptionMethod child of an EncryptedData element.

5. XML ENCRYPTION REQUIREMENTS

The following requirements for XML Encryption were defined:

- ➢ Users of an XML document that has encrypted content must be authorized. The processing system must be able to distinguish between authorized users and unauthorized users.
- ➢ There must be a means of individually encrypting elements within a single XML instance.
- ➢ XML content should be encrypted at creation of the XML document instance. XML document instances with encrypted elements should be saved encrypted when external to the repository.
- ➢ Elements with encrypted content must also be encrypted in any instance of the XML documents such that only authorized users can decrypt the encrypted content.
- ➢ The XML document should not require modification when an authorized user is added, deleted or modified.
- ➢ Must not interfere with the ability to digitally sign the document.

6. CONSIDERATIONS FOR XML ENCRYPTION

- ➢ Organizations typically define multiple categories when classifying the security requirements for their information. Banks have stringent security standards and typically define three broad categories:
    - a. Public – on disclosure no damage is done;
    - b. Confidential – on disclosure damage is minor and usually contained to an individual or causes minor financial loss; and
    - c. Sensitive – on disclosure damage is severe, may put national interests at risk or may cause great financial losses.
- ➢ There must be a way of designating an element or group of elements that needs to be protected without changing the original element or structure of the document (DTD);
- ➢ XML documents on the web may be retrieved through a variety of methods such as FTP, HTTP, HTTPS, e-mail, file sharing (directories), etc.

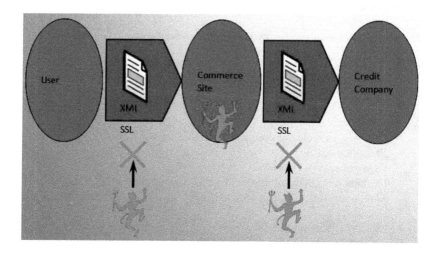

Figure 5 :- XML on SSL

7. AN INTRODUCTION TO XML ENCRYPTION

The Tokyo Research Lab has created the XML Security Suite, a prototype implementation of the XML signature specification. The XML Security Suite, available from IBM's alphaWorks, contains utilities to automatically generate XML digital signatures. When sending secure data across the Web, you need four things:

- o Confidentiality -- No one else can access or copy the data.
- o Integrity -- The data isn't altered as it goes from the sender to the receiver.
- o Authentication -- The document actually came from the purported sender.
- o Non-repudiability -- The sender of the data cannot deny that they sent it, and they cannot deny the contents of the data.

XML has become a repudiability valuable mechanism for data exchange across the Internet. SOAP, a means of sending XML messages, facilitates process intercommunication in ways not possible before.   Traditional methods of establishing trust between parties aren't appropriate on the public Internet or, indeed, on large LANs or WANs. In addition, the application of now standard security controls differentially to XML documents is not at all straightforward. An XML document, like any other, can be encrypted in its entirety and sent securely to one or more recipients.

This is a common function of SSL or TLS, for example, but what is much more interesting is how to handle situations where different parts of the same document need different treatment. A valuable benefit of XML is that a complete document can be sent as one operation and then held locally, thus reducing network traffic. But this then raises the question of how to control authorized viewing of different groups of elements. A researcher may need to be prevented from seeing personal details on medical records while an administrator may need exactly those details but should be prevented from viewing medical history; a doctor or nurse, in turn, may need medical details and some, but not all, personal material.

As with general encryption, there's no problem in digitally signing an XML document as a whole. However, difficulty arises when parts of a document need to be signed, perhaps by different people, and when this needs to be done in conjunction with selective encryption. signer view the item to be signed in plain text, and this may mean decrypting part of something already encrypted for other reasons. In other cases, data that is already encrypted may be encrypted further as part of a larger set.

There are additional problems, as well. One of the strengths of XML languages is that searching is clear and unambiguous: The DTD or schema provides information as to the relevant syntax. If a document subsection, including tags, is encrypted as a whole, then the ability to search for data relevant to those tags is lost. The core element in the XML encryption syntax is the Encrypted Data element which, with the Encrypted Key element, is used to transport encryption keys from the originator to a known recipient, and derives from the Encrypted Type abstract type. When an element or element content is encrypted, the Encrypted Data element replaces the element or content in the encrypted version of the XML document.

Though it is conceivable that XML Encryption could be used to encrypt any type of data, encryption of XML-encoded data is of special interest. This is because XML's ability to capture the structure and semantics of data unleashes new applications for the area of encryption. To this end, an important design consideration is to not encrypt more of an XML instance's structure and semantics than is necessary.

For example, suppose there is an XML instance containing a list of customers including their names, addresses, and credit card numbers. A contracted marketing employee may be entrusted to see the names and addresses but must not see the credit card number. If an application knows it should just be decrypting the content of <name>

elements, the XML instance needs to maintain its structure identifying what is a "name" and what isn't. Otherwise the application would have to decrypt the other data just to find out what it was supposed to be decrypting .

The centerpiece of XML Encryption is the <EncryptedNode> element. It has an attribute, NodeType, which indicates the type of node that was encrypted: element, element content, attribute, or attribute value. The encrypted node appears as a base64-encoded string, which forms the content of the <EncryptedNode> element.

Algorithm and keying information are captured in the <EncryptionInfo> element. Each <EncryptedNode> element has an associated <EncryptionInfo> element. The association my be accomplished by Pointing to the <EncryptionInfo> element through the EncryptionInfo attribute of the <EncryptedNode> element

When encrypting, applications create the <EncryptionInfo> element to store the information necessary for decryption. Multiple <EncryptedNode> elements may share a single <EncryptionInfo> element.

7.1 Symmetric XML Encryption

7.1.1. Intent

Encryption protects message confidentiality by making a message unreadable to those that do not have access to the key. Symmetric encryption uses the same key for encryption and decryption.

7.1.2 Example

Alice, in the Purchasing department regularly sends purchase orders to Bob in a distribution office. The purchase order contains sensitive data such as credit card numbers and other company information, so it is important to keep it secret. Eve can intercept her messages and may try to read them to get the confidential information.

7.1.3 Context

Applications that exchange sensitive information over insecure channels.

7.1.4 Problem

Applications that communicate with external applications interchange sensitive data that may be read by unauthorized users while they are in transit. How do we protect messages from being read by intruders? The solution for this problem is affected by the following forces: Confidentiality--Messages may be captured while they are in transit, so we need to prevent unauthorized users from reading them by hiding the information of the message. Hiding the information also makes replaying of messages by an attacker harder to perform. Reception--The hidden information should be revealed conveniently to the receiver.

Protocol--We need to apply the solution properly or it will not be able to stand attacks (there are several ways to attack a method to hide information.

Performance--The time to hide and recover the message should be reasonable.

7.1.5 Solution

So we need to prevent unauthorized users from reading them by hiding the information of the message using a symmetric cryptographic encryption. Transform a message in such a way that only can be understood by the intended receiver after applying the reverse transformation using a valid key. The transformation process at the sender's end is called Encryption, while the reverse transformation process at the receiver's end is called Decryption. The sender applies an encryption function (E) to the message (M) using a key (k); the output is the cipher text (C).

$$C = Ek\,(M)$$

When the cipher text (C) is delivered, the receiver applies a decryption function (D) to the cipher text using the same key (k) and recovers the message, i.e.

$$M = Dk\,(C)$$

A Principal may be a process, a user, or an organization that is responsible for sending or receiving messages. This Principal may have the roles of Sender or Receiver. A Sender may send a Message and/or a Encrypted Message to a receiver with which it shares a secret Key. The Encryptor creates the Encrypted Message that contain the cipher text using the shared key, while the Decryptor deciphers the encrypted data into its original form using the same key. Both the Encryptor and Decriptor use the same Algorithm to encipher and decipher a message. We describe the dynamic aspects of the Encryption Pattern using sequence diagrams for the following use cases: encrypt a message and decrypt a message.

Summary: A Sender wants to encrypt a message

Actors: A Sender

Precondition: Both sender and receiver have a shared key and access to a repository of algorithms. The message has already been created by the sender.

Description:
- A Sender sends the message, the shared key, and the algorithm identifier to the Encryptor.
- The Encryptor ciphers the message using the algorithm specified by the sender.
- The Encryptor creates the Encrypted Message that includes the cipher text.
- Postcondition: The message has been encrypted and sent to the sender.
- Summary: A receiver wants to decrypt an encrypted message from a sender.
- Actors: A Receiver
- Precondition: Both the sender and receiver have a shared key and access to a repository of algorithms.
- A Receiver sends the encrypted message and the shared key to the decryptor.
- The Decryptor deciphers the encrypted message using the shared key.
- The Decryptor creates the Message that contains the plain text obtained from the previous step.
- The Decryptor sends the plain Message to the receiver.
- Alternate Flows: If the key used in step b) is not the same as the one used for encryption, the decryption process fails.
- Postcondition: The encrypted message has been deciphered and delivered to the Receiver.

7.1.6 Implementation

> Use the Strategy Pattern [Gam94] to select different encryption algorithms.
> The designer should choose well-known algorithms such as AES (Advanced Encryption
> Standard) [Fed01] and DES (Data Encryption Standard) [Fed99]. Books such as
> Describe their features and criteria for selection.
> Encryption can be implemented in different applications such as in email communication, distribution of documents over the Internet, or web services. In these applications, we are able to encrypt the entire document. However, in web services we can encrypt parts of a message.
> Both the sender and the receiver have to previously agree what cryptographic algorithm
> They support a good key generator is very important. It should generate keys that are as random as possible or an attacker who captures some messages could be able to deduce the key..
> A long encryption key should be used (at least 64 bits). Only brute force is known to work against the DES and AES for example; using a short key would let the attacker generate all possible keys.

7.1.7 Known Uses

Symmetric Encryption has been widely used in different products. GNuPG [Gnu] is free software that secures data from eavesdroppers. OpenSSL [Ope] is an open source toolkit that encrypts and decrypts files. Java Cryptographic Extension [Sun] provides a framework and implementations for encryption. The .NET framework [Mica] provides several classes to perform encryption and decryption using symmetric algorithms. XML Encryption [W3C02] is one of the foundation web services security standards that defines the structure and process of encryption for XML messages. Pretty Good Privacy (PGP), a set of programs used mostly for e-mail security, includes methods for symmetric encryption and decryption [PGP].

7.1.8 Consequences

This pattern presents the following advantages:

Only receivers who possess the shared key can decrypt a message transforming it into a readable form. A captured message is unreadable to the attacker. This makes attacks based on replaying a message very hard. The strength of a cryptosystem is based on the secrecy of a long key. The cryptographic algorithms are known to the public, so the key should be kept protected from unauthorized users. It is possible to select from several encryption algorithms the one suitable for the application needs. There exist encryption algorithms that take a reasonable time to encrypt messages. The pattern also has some (possible) liabilities.

This pattern assumes that the shared key was distributed in a secure way. This may not be easy for large groups of nodes exchanging messages. Cryptography operations are computationally intensive and may affect the performance of the application.

Encryption does not provide data integrity. The encrypted data can be modified by an attacker, and the receiver would decrypt the cipher text to something else other than the original text. Encryption does not prevent a replay attack because an encrypted message can be captured and resent without being decrypted. It is recommended to use another security mechanism such as Timestamps or Nonce.

7.1.9 Example resolved

Alice, in the Purchasing department encrypts the purchase orders she sends to Bob. The purchase's order sensitive data is now unreadable to Eve. Eve can try to apply to it all possible keys but if the algorithm has been well implemented, she cannot read the confidential information.

7.1.10 Related Patterns

Information Secrecy Pattern [Bra98], supports the encryption/decryption of data. This pattern describes encryption in more general terms. It does not distinguish between asymmetric and symmetric encryption.
Strategy Pattern [Gam94], defines how to separate the implementation of related algorithms from the selection of one of them.

7.2 XML Encryption Pattern

7.2.1 Intent

XML Encryption standard [W3C02] describes the syntax to represent XML encrypted data and the process of encryption and decryption. XML Encryption provides message confidentiality by hiding sensitive information in such way that can be understood only by intended recipients.

7.2.2 Example

Alice, in the Purchasing department regularly sends purchase orders in the form of XML documents to Bob, who works in a distribution office. The purchase order contains sensitive data such as credit card numbers and other company information, so it is important to keep it secret. In the receiving end, different people will handle different parts of the order. Eve can intercept these orders and may try to read them to get the confidential information.

7.2.3 Context

Users of web services send and receive SOAP messages through insecure networks such as the Internet.

7.2.2. Problem

Applications that communicate with external applications or users interchange sensitive data that may be read by unauthorized people while the messages with this data are in transit. The solution for this problem is affected by the following forces:

Messages may be captured while they are in transit, so we need to prevent unauthorized users from reading them by hiding the information of the message using encryption.

We need to express encrypted elements in a standardized XML format to allow encrypted data to be nested within an XML message. Otherwise, different applications cannot interoperate. Different parts of a message may be intended for different recipients, and not all the information contained within a message should be available to all the recipients. Thus, recipients should be able to read only those parts of the message that are intended for them. For flexibility reasons, both symmetric and asymmetric encryption algorithms should be supported.

If a secret key is embedded in the message, it should be protected. Otherwise, an attacker could read some messages.

7.2.3. Solution

Transform a message using some algorithm so that it can only be understood by legitimate receivers that possess a valid key. First, the data has to be serialized before encryption. The serialization process will convert the data into octets. Then, this serialized data is encrypted using the chosen algorithm and the encryption key. The cipher data and the information of the encryption (algorithm, key, and other properties) are represented in XML format.

XML Encryption supports both types of encryption: symmetric and asymmetric. The symmetric encryption algorithm uses a common key for both encryption and decryption. On the other hand, the asymmetric encryption algorithm uses a key pair (public key and private key). The sender encrypts a message using the receiver's public key, and the receiver uses its private key to decrypt the encrypted message. Thus, in both types of encryption, only recipients who possess the shared key or the private key that matches the public key used in the encryption process can read the encrypted message after decryption.

A Principal may be a process, a system, a user, or an organization that sends and receives XMLMessages and/or EncryptedXMLMessages. This principal may have the roles of Sender and Receiver. Both an XMLMessage and a EncryptedMLMessage are composed of XML elements. Each XMLElement may have many children, and each child also can be composed by other XML elements, and so on. The Encryptor and the Decryptor encipher a message and decipher an encrypted message respectively.

The EncryptedData contains other subelements such as the encryption method, key information, cipher value, and encryption properties. The Encryption Method is an optional element that specifies the algorithm used to encrypt the data. If this element is not specified, the receiver must know the encryption algorithm. The KeyInfo (optional) contains the same key information as the one describes in the XML Signature standard [W3C08]. However, this standard defines two other subelements: EncryptedKey and ReferenceList. The EncryptedKey contains similar elements as the EncryptedData; however, they are not shown in the class diagram.

The EncryptedKey includes an optional ReferenceList element that points to data or keys encrypted using this key. The CipherData is a mandatory element that stores either the cipher value or a pointer (cipher reference) where the encrypted data is located. The Encryption Properties element holds information such as the time that the encryption was performed or the serial number of the hardware used for this process.

Dynamics: We describe the dynamic aspects of the XML Encryption Pattern using sequence diagrams for the following use cases: "encrypt XML elements" and "decrypt an encrypted XML message".

Summary: A sender wants to encrypt different elements of an XML message using a shared key.

Actors: A sender

Precondition: Both sender and receiver have a shared key and a list of encryption algorithms.

Description:

- A sender requests to the encryptor to encrypt a list of XML elements. This list is
- Represented with an asterisk (*) in the sequence diagram.
- The encryptor creates the EncryptedXMLMessage.
- The encryptor encrypts the XML Element using the shared key and the encryption
- Method provided by the sender and produces an encrypted value.
- The encryptor creates the EncryptionData element including the EncryptionMethod that
- holds the encryption algorithm used to encrypt the data, the KeyInfo that contains
- information about the key, and the CipherData obtained from step c)
- The encryptor replaces the XML element with the encrypted data.
- Repeat steps c) to e) for each XML element to encrypt.
- The encryptor sends the EncrypteXMLMessage to the sender.

Alternate Flows: none

Postcondition: The encrypted XML message has been created.
Summary: A receiver wants to decrypt an encrypted XML message.

Actors: A Receiver

Precondition: Both sender and receiver have a shared key and a list of encryption algorithms

Description:

- A receiver requests to the verifier to decrypt an encrypted XML message.
- The decryptor creates the XMLMessage that contains a copy of the
- EncryptedXMLMessage.
- The decryptor obtains the elements within the EncryptedData element such as the
- EncryptionMethod, KeyInfo, and the cipherValue.
- The encryptor decrypts the cipher value using the encryption method and the shared key.
- The encryptor replaces the encrypted data with the plain text obtained from the previous step.
- Repeat steps c) to e) for each XML element to decrypt.
- The decryptor sends the decrypted XMLMessage to the receiver.

Alternate Flows:

If the key used in step d) is not the same as the one used in the encryption, then the decryption process fails.

Postcondition: The message has been decrypted.

7.2.4. Implementation:

The designer should choose strong encryption algorithm to prevent attackers from breaking them such as Advanced Encryption Standard (AES) and DES (Data Encryption Standard) for symmetric encryption and RSA (Rivest, Shamir, and Adleman) for asymmetric encryption. Asymmetric encryption or public-key encryption is more computationally intensive than symmetric encryption. However, symmetric encryption requires that both sender and receiver share a common key. A better practice will be to use the asymmetric encryption in combination with the symmetric encryption. Use symmetric encryption for the data and asymmetric encryption for secure key distribution. XML Encryption supports both symmetric and asymmetric encryption. This provides application flexibility; for example, a session uses symmetric encryption and key distribution uses asymmetric encryption.

7.2.5. Known Uses

Several vendors have developed tools that support XML Encryption:
Xtradyne's Web Service Domain Boundary Controller (WS-DBC) [Xtr]. The WS-DBC
is an XML firewall that provides protection against malformed messages and malicious
content, XML encryption, XML signature, and authentication, authorization, and audit.
IBM - DataPower XML Security Gateway XS40 [IBM] parses, filters, validates schema,
decrypts, verifies signatures, signs, and encrypts XML message flows. Forum Systems -
Forum Sentry SOA Gateway [For] conforms to XML Digital Signature, XML
Encryption, WS-Trust, WS-Policy and other standards. Microsoft .NET [Mic] includes
APIs that support the encryption and decryption of XML data.

7.2.6. Consequences

This pattern presents the following advantages:
Only users that know the key can decrypt and read the message. Each recipient can only
decrypt parts of a message that are intended for him but are unable to decrypt the rest.
The EncryptedData is an XML element that replaces the data to be encrypted.
The EncryptedData as well as the EncryptedKey are composed by other subelements
such as encryption method, key information, and cipher value. The entire XML message
or only some parts can be encrypted.
If both the sender and the receiver have not exchanged the keys previously, the key can
be sent in the message encrypted using public key system.

The pattern also has some (possible) liabilities:

The structure is rather complex and users may get confused.

7.2.7. Related Patterns

This pattern is a specialization of the Symmetric Encryption Pattern. WS-
Security Pattern [Has09] is a standard for securing XML messages using XML
signature, XML Encryption, and security tokens. Strategy Pattern [Gam94] defines
how to separate the implementation of related algorithms from the selection of one of
them.
The following specifications are related to XML Signature, but they have not
been developed as patterns.

The XML Key Management Specification (XKMS) [W3C01] specifies the distribution and registration of public keys, and works together with XML Encryption. WS-SecurityPolicy [OAS07] standard describes how to express security policies such as what algorithms are supported by a web service or what parts of an incoming message need to be signed or encrypted.

7.3 Proposed Approach

The objective of XML is to use a structured approach to provide searchable content in documents. The problem with using an element for encryption is that it does not promote an understanding of the structure of the document which could lead to confusion and not permit the ability to search the structure or specific content based on tags. If we have multiple elements that need encrypting we lose the ability to search these elements using the elements of the structure of the DTD or schema.

In the interest of maintaining the existing structure of documents and not have to create a special element for encryption that may not promote understanding/search ability within the structure of the document it is proposed that W3C XML Encryption use element attributes to describe elements that should be protected. In this way multiple levels of classification could be assigned to elements within a document.

7.4 A Sample Document – Medical XML

XML medical record document has confidential and sensitive information divided into four basic components (I could have created four different security classifications but decided to use only two for this example):

- ✓ Personal information - name, address etc about the person - confidential
- ✓ Billing information - credit card, history - confidential
- ✓ Medical characteristics - age, height, weight, etc - sensitive
- ✓ Medical history - case information - sensitive

XSL document, Med7.xsl, is used to display the desired content. The level of security in this sample could be mapped to three different requirements:

1.) Doctor: - who needs to see all the information
2.) Billing clerk: - who needs to see the personal and billing information only
3.) Researcher: - who needs to see the medical characteristics and history only.

The point of encrypting the content relates to the ability to send the information via e-mail and maintain the confidentiality of the information until it reaches the destination (users system) and the user decrypts the information. This is as opposed to SSL which decrypts the information at the server and the information is then unencrypted, internal to the organization where is has the potential of being intercepted.

7.4.1 XML Document – Patient Medical Record

The XML document has four parts that need to be protected from unauthorized access. These are identified by using "class = 'confidential | sensitive'". In this sample the data would be extracted from a protected database and encrypted using a symmetric key(s) prior to being inserted into the XML instance. Access controls could be PKI, PGP, flat file (another XML document) or a database. A program or script will be required to link the user to the access requirements and encrypt the symmetric key with the users public key or some other method of ensuring unique and secure transport of the encrypted content. The sample below provides a high level view of the file without getting into the details of how the encryption and access controls are done.

7.4.3 Sample XML Medical Record File

<?xml version="1.0" encoding="UTF-8" ?>

<!-- program to look at ACL (Access Control List either LDAP, PGP, file or Database) to determine authorized users and access requirements, encrypts confidential key and/or sensitive key with public key (asymmetric key) or some other means to uniquely identify the user and access control-->

<MedicalRecord>

<Personal class="confidential">

 <FirstName>Mark</FirstName>

 <Address>

```
<Street1>100 Bent Road</Street1>

<city>Los Angeles</city>

<stateProvince>California</stateProvince>

<country>USA</country>

<ZIP_Postal>123456</ZIP_Postal>

</Address>

</Personal>
<Billing_Information class="confidential">
<Credit_card class="confidential">

        <card_type class="confidential">VISA</card_type>

<Expiry_date>02/02</Expiry_date>

<card_number class="confidential">4404 5505 6606 7707</card_number>

</Credit_card>

<Account_history class="confidential">Invoice Number 124 amount $2,000 Paid
VISA</Account_history>

</Billing_Information>
<Medical_characteristics class="sensitive">

<DateOfBirth>19610707</DateOfBirth>

<Age>39</Age>

<Sex>Male</Sex>

</Medical_characteristics>
```

```
<Medical_history class="sensitive">

<CASE class="sensitive">

 <Date>19870606</Date>

 <Symptom class="sensitive">stomach craps, vomiting, drowsy, incoherent</Symptom>

 <Treatment class="sensitive">Pumped stomach, overdose of sleeping pills</Treatment>

 </CASE>

 </Medical_history>

 </MedicalRecord>
```

7.4.4 XSL Sample Stylesheet

The XSL stylesheet demonstrates that content can be hidden based on the security classification of the information. In this case the sensitive information will not be displayed.

```
<?xml version='1.0'?>

<!-- access control program to authenticate authorized user and use access control requirements within XSL stylesheet to determine what the user is allowed to see-->

<xsl:stylesheet xmlns:xsl='http://www.w3.org/XSL/Transform/1.0'>

<xsl:template match = "/MedicalRecord">

<HTML> <HEAD><TITLE>Medical Record</TITLE></HEAD>

<BODY>

<H2>Medical Records</H2>
```

<!-- XSL commands that use the access control parameters from the above access control program to determine access privileges of user and to remove any content that user is not authorized to see-->

<UL>

<H3>Personal Information</H3>

<xsl:apply-templates select="Personal"/>

<font color="green">

<H3>Billing Information</H3>

<xsl:apply-templates select="Billing_Information"/>

</font></UL></BODY></HTML>

</xsl:template>

<xsl:template match="Medical_characteristics[@class ='sensitive']"/>

</xsl:template>

<xsl:template match="Medical_history[@class ='sensitive']"/>

</xsl:template></xsl:stylesheet>

8. KEY ISSUES WITH XML ENCRYPTION

There are a number of key issues that must be addressed with XML Encryption:
1)   Access control – determine who is authorized to see what
2)   Protection of content

8.1 Access Control

-       Access control should perform two functions:

-       identify who has access

- determine what the authorized user can see

The creation step of XML would require some means of uniquely identifying the user(s) using some sort of Access Control List (ACL) that provides a number of key pieces of information such as:

- Contact information (e-mail or location)

- Level of access (is the person authorized to see all)

- Unique identifier (ensures that that person is uniquely identified)

8.2 Protection of Data:

Sensitive or confidential information should be protected at all times outside the source. At creation of the XML instance the content that is deemed confidential or sensitive should be encrypted prior to insertion into the instance. In the example the data would be encrypted using a symmetric key or keys depending on the number of levels of security required. The encrypted information within the created instance should remain encrypted when the user is not viewing the information. It should be saved in encrypted format to remove the risk of having the content available to unauthorized users in the event that the authorized user leaves his/her workstation unattended or the system is lost or stolen.

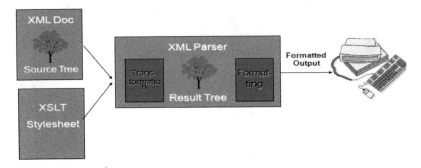

Fig 6:- XML Processing Model

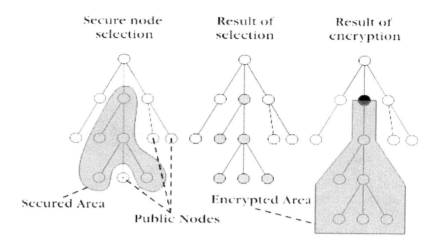

Fig.07 :- Encryption Node identification

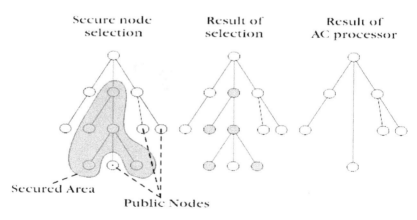

Fig.08 :- Encryption Node Selection

9. EXAMPLES

The examples in this section illustrate how XML Encryption would work in a variety of scenarios.

9.1 Encrypt an entire element

The plaintext:

<root>...

<ElementToBeEncrypted Attr1="Value1" Attr2="Value2" ...>

...</ElementToBeEncrypted>

...</root>

when secured becomes

<root>...

<EncryptionInfo xmlns="http://www.w3.org/2001/03/Encryption

   Id="encryptionInfo23"...>

   <EncryptionInfo>...<EncryptedNode xmlns="http://www.w3.org/2001/03/Encryption"

   NodeType="Element"   EncryptionInfo="#encryptionInfo23">

   (Base64 of encrypted Element node)

</EncryptedNode> ...</root>

9.2 Encrypt content of an element but not the element itself

Scenario: As mentioned earlier, in many applications it makes sense NOT to unnecessarily encrypt the structure and semantics of an XML instance. In this case, an application wants to keep secret just the content of an element.

```
<root>

...<EncryptionInfo xmlns="http://www.w3.org/2001/03/Encryption

  Id="encryptionInfo23"...>  </EncryptionInfo>

...<Element Attr1="Value1" Attr2="Value2" Attr3="Value3">

  <EncryptedNodexmlns="http://www.w3.org/2001/03/Encryption"
  NodeType="ElementContent"    EncryptionInfo="#encryptionInfo23">

    (Base64 of encrypted element content)

  </EncryptedNode>

</Element>

...</root>
```

10. SECURITY

The XML Encryption specification must include a discussion of potential vulnerabilities and recommended practices when using the defined processing model in a larger application context. While it is impossible to predict all the ways an XML Encryption standard may be used, the discussion should alert users to ways in which potentially subtle weaknesses might be introduced.

At a minimum, the following types of vulnerabilities must be addressed.

1.   Security issues arising from known plain-text and data length information An attacker may know the original structure of the plain text via its schema. An attacker may know the length and redundancy of the plain-text data.

2.   Processing of invalid decrypted data if an integrity checking mechanism is not used in conjunction with encryption.

3.   Potential weaknesses resulting from combining signing and encryption operations.

4.   Sign before you encrypt: the signature may reveal information about the data that has now been encrypted unless proper precautions are taken (such as properly adding an encrypted random string to the plaintext before hashing).

5.   The specification should warn application designers and users about revealing information about the encrypted data

11. XML DIGITAL SIGNATURE

Digital signatures use cryptographic techniques to protect the integrity of information. The key used to sign data is typically controlled by a single entity and so the creation of a signature can be directly traced to the owner of the key. The validation of a signature includes not only the cryptographic processing, but also the determination that a key was trusted to sign a specific piece of information. The trust in a key is determined by the validation of other signed statements, or certificates, that describe the appropriate usage of the public key.

XML Digital Signature provides integrity, message authentication, and/or signer authentication services for data of any type, whether located within the XML that includes the signature or elsewhere.

XML Security Library supports all MUST/SHOULD/MAY features and algorithms described in the W3C standard and provide API to sign prepared document templates, add signature(s) to a document "on-the-fly" or verify the signature(s) in the document.

XML Digital Signature Online Verifier is an example of a real application based on XML Security Library. Using this tool you can verify any XML Signature and get detailed report on what and how was signed.

11.1 How is the validity of an XML digital signature determined?

The following steps determine the cryptographic correctness of a digital signature:

1) Use the cryptographic algorithm parameter definitions in the signature to determine: the appropriate hash algorithm, signature algorithm, signature format, asymmetric algorithm parameters and public key to use in the validation process.

2) Use the appropriate hash algorithm on a canonical representation of the signed data.

3) Use the appropriate algorithms and public key to create a digital signature over the hashed information.

4) Compare the newly computed signature to the attached signature. The validation fails at this point if they are not the same.

5) Determine if the public key used to create the signature was trusted for this specific signature application.

11.2 Recommendations

Signed XML should provide a means to not only sign a resource, but to also carry information that supports the evaluation of the signature semantics. Signed XML should provide mechanisms to support the complete validation of digital signatures. This validation needs to include the processing of constraints on key usage specific to an application. These constraints are best expressed in XML.

12. BIBLOGRAPHY

- www.w3.org/Encryption/2001

- www.w3.org/TR/xmlenc-core

- www.106.ibm.com/developerworks/xml/library/x-encrypt

- www.aleksey.com/xmlsec/xmlenc.html

- www.xml.com/pub/r/1091